Drawn
to the Gospels

An Illustrated Lectionary

JAY SIDEBOTHAM

CHURCH
PUBLISHING
INCORPORATED

□ □ □

This book is dedicated to Frances,
who after many years of marriage remains kind enough
to chuckle at my cartoons.

□ □ □

Church Publishing
19 East 34th Street
New York, NY 10016

www.churchpublishing.org

Cover art by Jay Sidebotham
Cover design by Jennifer Kopec, 2Pug Design
Typeset by Denise Hoff

Library of Congress Cataloging-in-Publication Data

Names: Sidebotham, Jay, author.
Title: Drawn to the Gospels : an illustrated lectionary (Year C) / Jay Sidebotham.
Description: New York : Church Publishing, 2018.
Identifiers: LCCN 2018014951 (print) | LCCN 2018029056 (ebook) |
    ISBN 9781640650855 (ebook) | ISBN 9781640650848 (pbk.)
Subjects: LCSH: Bible. Gospels--Meditations. | Church year meditations. |
    Common lectionary (1992). Year C.
Classification: LCC BS2555.54 (ebook) | LCC BS2555.54 .S546 2018 (print) |
    DDC 264/.34--dc23
LC record available at https://lccn.loc.gov/2018014951

Printed in the United States of America

CONTENTS

INTRODUCTION
How Would You
Tell the Story of Jesus?

What part of the story would you emphasize? What do you think is most important for people to know about Jesus? Evidently, telling the story of Jesus is something we're all supposed to do. In the service of Holy Baptism, the following question is asked of the whole congregation:

Will you proclaim by word and example the Good News of God in Christ?

It is a promise that we will share the Good News of Jesus as we know it, a promise that we will tell the story. There are lots of ways to do that. This book is just one of them, as it moves us through the church year, beginning with the First Sunday in Advent. For each Sunday, we include a cartoon to illustrate something about the portion of the gospel to be read in church, a few comments about the reading, and some questions to think about.

It's exciting that there's more than one way to tell this story. We give thanks in particular for the four gospels in the New Testament, and the varied ways that they share the story of Jesus.

What About the Cover of This Book?

For a long time, the Church has recognized the distinctive voices of the gospels and represented them with ancient symbols: Matthew is represented as a human being; Mark as a lion; Luke as an ox; and John as an eagle. Each character is depicted with wings, indicating the presence and participation of God in the writing of the gospels. The symbols, depicted on the cover, have biblical roots. We read about four such figures in the Book of Ezekiel (chapter 1) and also in the Revelation to John (4:6–9ff).

As you might imagine, commentators over the centuries have offered various interpretations of what these symbols mean, some more far fetched than others. For example, the symbol of Matthew—a winged man, or perhaps an angel—represents the humanity of Jesus, noting the way that the gospel begins with the genealogy of Jesus. The symbol of Mark—a lion—suggests a figure of courage and monarchy, as Jesus announces the nearness of the Realm of God. The symbol of Luke—an ox—reflects a figure of sacrifice, service, and strength. The symbol of John—an eagle—may represent the soaring, poetic language of the gospel, or the persistent and paradoxical theme in John's gospel that Jesus comes from above and returns to his heavenly realm when he is "lifted up," lifted up on the cross, lifted up to heaven.

At various times in the history of the Church, efforts have been made to harmonize, and even homogenize the gospels. The *Diatessaron*, a document created by an ascetic named Tatian in the second century, is one of the earliest examples of this kind of attempt. The Church over the centuries decided to let four distinct voices stand, even if and when they disagree (and they sometimes do).

The Church has also decided that it is important for us to hear each of these voices. So we worship on Sunday guided by a three-year lectionary (the Revised Common Lectionary), a schedule of readings used by many denominations. On any given Sunday, you could drop in on a church down the street or on the other side of the globe and hear the same readings that are being read at your home church.

The lectionary is designed for a year-long focus on each of three gospels, Matthew, Mark, or Luke. They have been called the *synoptic gospels*, which literally means that they can be seen together, or alongside each other in parallel tracks (*syn,* being a prefix meaning "with"; *optic,* having to do with being seen). These three gospels follow a similar outline and share a great deal of material, though each one contains some writings that are unique. In the course of the three lectionary years, we read a good chunk of the Gospel of John, which follows a different outline and represents a different style of writing with a distinctive theological perspective on the story of Jesus.

Which Brings Us to the Gospel of Luke . . .

This year in church (Year C), we will focus on the third gospel, attributed to Luke, a master storyteller who provides us with a number of insights into the life of Jesus that we might not otherwise have. Take a minute to look at the way that Luke begins his gospel. In the first sentences, he addresses the letter to someone named Theophilus, which means "God-lover." Theophilus could be a real individual or a generic title for anyone interested in knowing more about God. In the opening verses, Luke suggests that he had had a chance to see various accounts of the story of Jesus. Having seen them, he feels called to write his own "orderly account." It makes one wonder if he thought the other accounts were not sufficiently orderly. He brings his considerable gifts as a historian and storyteller to the task of explaining who Jesus is and what the Jesus movement is all about.

The tradition around Luke is rich. He is identified as a Gentile. He traveled around the Mediterranean with Paul, which must have had joys and challenges. His writing style suggests education. And he was prolific. He wrote not only this gospel but also the Acts of the Apostles, which means, in terms of word count, that he is responsible for about 25 percent of the New Testament. A doctor by profession, he emphasizes healing. We can tell by his writings that he cared deeply about the power of the Spirit and a life of prayer. A renaissance kind of guy, he is known as the patron saint of artists. He has a heart for those who were outsiders in his culture: women, Samaritans, those who were poor. He believes that these folks were on the receiving end of God's grace, so that the gospel has universal scope. He believes that the least among us have something to teach us, lessons often conveyed in parables like the Good Samaritan, where the outsider becomes the hero. That story and the parable of the Prodigal Son appear only in Luke's gospel. We are indebted to Luke for these classic stories of grace, forgiveness, and healing. As you read his gospel throughout the year, we will do our best to note his unique contributions to the gospel, as we give thanks that he decided to offer his orderly account of the story of Jesus.

Which Brings Us to This Book . . .

It is clear that, in the Christian tradition, spiritually vital congregations and spiritually vital individuals engage with the Bible on some level. The Prayer Book recommends that we read, hear, learn, mark, and inwardly digest scripture. There are many ways to do that. This book and its companions for the other two years of the lectionary cycle offer one way to go deeper with the gospel reading you hear on Sunday.

For each Sunday in the year, we include a cartoon drawing—one person's perspective on the story. Some of the cartoons are silly. Some are slightly irreverent. They are offered to bring the gospel passage to life, and they are offered with a light touch, in the spirit of G.K. Chesterton, who said that angels could fly because they take themselves lightly. Then we include a paragraph of commentary, followed by a few questions.

How to Use This Book

You might use it for your own personal devotion, as a way to get ready for Sunday or as a way to reflect on the gospel passage after you have been to church and heard a compelling, or maybe not so compelling, sermon. You might want to use the book in your home with your family. Perhaps after dinner, you might read the passage and answer a couple of the questions and then talk about the drawing, or even add to it.

You might want to copy the drawings and put them in the church bulletin, or have them on individual sheets or even posters, for children (of all ages) to color. You might use the book as a resource in Sunday school classes, Bible studies, or Confirmation classes. Some adults even seem to enjoy the drawings. Others may enjoy coloring them, since adult coloring books seem to be all the rage.

You may find the questions helpful, and you may need to translate them for use with different groups. If the questions provided are not working for you, here is another way to think about each gospel passage. Ask these two simple questions, which can be applied to almost any gospel passage:

1. Who is Jesus in this passage?

2. What does this passage tell us about what it means to be one of his followers?

You may want to simply read the gospel and ask about the so-what factor: What difference does this gospel passage make in my week?

Mother Teresa is revered and remembered for many reasons. Among her many vocations was a deep love of scripture. She taught that we are called to know the word, love the word, live the word, and give the word. This book of often silly drawings is offered with the serious intent that the story of Jesus might become a part of who we are in a world that desperately needs to know more about God's grace and love.

ADVENT

The First Sunday in Advent
Luke 21:25-36

Notes on This Reading

Happy New Year. The church begins its new year not on January 1, but on the first Sunday in Advent. The readings for the day come not from the beginning of Luke's gospel, but from one of the gospel's last chapters. The passage anticipates Jesus's arrival, not showing up in the manger in Bethlehem, but descending from the clouds in great glory. All of which makes us sit up and take notice. The theme of Advent is clear. We are called to be on guard, to be alert, to be ready. We'll spend the next four weeks, in advance of Christmas, trying to figure out what that means.

Questions

1. How does this passage make you feel? Is it scary, or exciting, or strange?

2. Why do you think that we begin the church year with this reading about apocalyptic end times? What does the word "apocalyptic" suggest to you?

3. What do you think it means that the kingdom of God, or the realm of God, is near? Where do you see the realm of God in your own life?

4. What will you do in the coming weeks of Advent to get ready for Christ's coming?

The Second Sunday in Advent
Luke 3:1-6

Notes on This Reading

John the Baptist has a starring role in the season of Advent, but we read about him not only in this season but also in other parts of the year. That's one way of letting us know that he is a significant biblical figure. Jesus, at one point, called him the greatest person born of a woman. We are called to pay attention to what he says. His ministry was one of preparation, getting the way ready for Christ to come into the world, and getting himself out of the way. There's a lot that is surprising about John the Baptist, but Luke tells us we should not be too surprised. His ministry was predicted by the prophet Isaiah, hundreds of years earlier.

Questions

1. Why do you think John the Baptist gets so much airtime in the New Testament?

2. When have you been in the wilderness, literally or figuratively? What can be learned in such a place?

3. What does it look like to prepare the way of the Lord? How might you do that this week? How might you do that in this Advent season?

The Third Sunday in Advent
Luke 3:7-18

Notes on This Reading

Here is John the Baptist again, and a sampling of his distinctive style of preaching. He doesn't sugarcoat his message. How often have you heard a preacher begin by calling the congregation a "brood of vipers"? He definitely raises the stakes and invites people to think about their own lives. What are they doing with what they have been given? How are they treating each other? Those are good questions for all of us to consider. A side note: The passage ends by saying John was proclaiming good news. If that's the good news, one wonders what the bad news would sound like.

Questions

1. What does it mean to bear fruit worthy of repentance?

2. What might those fruits look like in your life?

3. In verses 10–14, John the Baptist gives some specific ethical guidelines. Do any of them apply to your life?

4. John the Baptist is often depicted in paintings with arm extended, pointing to Jesus? Why do you think that is so? What does it mean for us to point to Jesus?

5. How is his hard-hitting message good news?

The Fourth Sunday in Advent
Luke 1:39-45 (46-55)

Notes on This Reading

Thanks be to Luke for giving us this story of the meeting between two relatives, Mary and Elizabeth—one young, one old, both unexpectedly expecting children, both faithful women who end up as mothers of main characters in the New Testament. Both will lose their sons in an untimely and violent manner. Mary's hymn, the Magnificat, is one of the treasures of the New Testament. It has woven its way into the liturgy of the Episcopal Church, as it offers a message of expectation and hope.

Questions

1. How do you think Elizabeth feels about this encounter with her younger cousin?

2. How would you describe Mary, based on the song she sings?

3. What does it mean to magnify the Lord?

4. Some have said that the Magnificat is an echo of the Song of Hannah (1 Samuel 2). Compare and contrast these two hymns.

CHRISTMAS

Christmas Day: The Nativity of Our Lord Jesus Christ: Proper I and II
Luke 2:1-20

Notes on This Reading

Again, we have Luke to thank for details we would not otherwise know: things like the census, or no room in the inn, or the news announced to the shepherds. Think of all the carols we would be missing without this information. Luke tells what is now a familiar story. Our challenge is to hear it as if for the first time. It's an amazing story of the announcement of new life beginning in dire circumstances, about greatness emerging from humble beginnings. Celebrate that good news! It's a gift!

Questions

1. Imagine you have never heard this story before. That's hard to do, but what do you think would be most striking?

2. What is the significance of the fact that there was no room for the young couple in the inn?

3. Why do you think shepherds were the first to receive this news?

4. What do you think Mary was pondering in particular? Put yourself in her place.

Christmas Day:
The Nativity of Our Lord
Jesus Christ: Proper III
John 1:1-14 (15-18)

Notes on This Reading

(This reading is also selected for the First Sunday after Christmas.)

There are all kinds of ways to tell the Christmas story. Mark doesn't talk at all about the circumstances of Jesus's birth. Matthew and Luke both take us back to Bethlehem, with shepherds and angels and such. John goes back even further to the beginning of creation, with words echoing the opening words of the book of Genesis: in the beginning. It is as if to say that the story of Jesus, the story about to be told in his gospel, rivals the story of creation in significance. How amazing is that? These verses have been called the prologue to the gospel. Think of this passage as an overture, hitting themes that will be repeated throughout the pages that follow. Note the themes as they reappear in the gospel.

Questions

1. What does it mean that the beginning of the gospel has to do with the Word?

2. How is the Christmas story about that kind of communication?

3. Why do you think John the Baptist gets a shout-out?

4. In verses 10–13, how is the story of Jesus summarized?

5. What is your favorite way to tell the story of Christmas?

The Feast of the Holy Name
Luke 2:15-21

Notes on This Reading

What's in a name? Luke is the only gospel that tells us about the ways that Mary and Joseph fulfill the commitments of their tradition to name their child eight days after birth. The name that was given to the child is Jesus, loaded with significance because it means "God saves." It is so significant that the event gets its own feast day in the church calendar: January 1.

Questions

1. When Luke tells us that Mary treasured these words and pondered all these things in her heart, what do you imagine was going on in her head? What were the range of emotions she might have been experiencing?

2. What is so significant about a name? Why did you receive the name you were given?

3. What does it mean that Jesus's parents fulfilled the religious traditions of their day?

4. When in the New Testament, people call on the name of Jesus, what do you think that means?

The Second Sunday
after Christmas
Matthew 2:13-15, 19-23

Notes on This Reading

This Sunday, we are given a choice. We can stay with Luke or we can choose to take a detour and dive into the Gospel of Matthew, the only gospel that tells this story of Joseph, Mary, and Jesus making their way to Egypt. Just as the children of Israel were protected and preserved in the Book of Genesis when Joseph went down to Egypt, the promised child is protected from the cruelty of Herod by a journey to Egypt. Matthew's gospel will, in fact, present Jesus as a new kind of Moses, bringing a new kind of law or teaching. Think of other ways that Jesus might be like Moses.

Questions

1. Have you ever had a dream that provided guidance for you?

2. The word "angel" really means messenger. Have you had any angels in your life, giving guidance about where you should go or what you should do?

3. Can you imagine how Joseph and Mary felt as they fled their homeland?

4. Imagine how people feel these days when in different parts of the world, they need to leave homeland for the sake of safety. Think especially of what it must be like to move with young children. Say prayers for those who are refugees this day. Maybe there is some way you can help them.

The Second Sunday after Christmas

Luke 2:15–52

(an alternative reading)

Notes on This Reading

On this Sunday, we can either read the passage from Matthew's gospel (see the previous entry) or we can read from the Gospel of Luke, repeating some of what was read on January 1, the Feast of the Holy Name. But the story continues on this Sunday, introducing us to two amazing characters. (If perchance, this reading doesn't get airtime in your church, it will be read again on February 2, the Feast of the Presentation.) Only Luke tells us about Simeon and Anna, two elderly people who believed God would let them see the fulfillment of promises they had waited their whole lives to see. When the eight-day-old baby Jesus is brought to the temple, old Simeon catches a glimpse of him, and breaks into a song of praise which we still use in our Book of Common Prayer. Similarly, Anna, a faithful, elderly woman, celebrates fulfillment of the promise. We give thanks to Luke for introducing us to these two faithful people, who challenge us to trust in God, who model patience and faithfulness.

Questions

1. How good are you at waiting? What do you think Anna and Simeon were waiting for?

2. What did they notice in the infant Jesus?

3. When the gospel tells us that Mary treasured these things in her heart, what do you think she was thinking about in this particular meeting?

4. When Simeon told her a sword would pierce her heart, what do you imagine she thought about that?

5. What do you make of the story of Jesus teaching folks in the temple as a young adolescent?

6. When Luke tells us that Jesus grew in wisdom and stature, it suggests he changed. Can you think of other times Jesus changed?

The Second Sunday after Christmas, and the Feast of the Epiphany
Matthew 2:1-12

Notes on This Reading

On those rare occasions when there are two Sundays in the season of Christmas, we can turn to the story of the magi, who come from the east, following a star leading them to the child born in Bethlehem. Only Matthew tells us this story—the story of the Epiphany. We read it not only on this Second Sunday of Christmas, which, because of the calendar does not happen all that often. We also read it on the Feast of the Epiphany, January 6, a great celebration that launches a whole new season, filled with stories about how people come to see who Jesus is.

Questions

1. Why do you think Herod and the people of Jerusalem were frightened? How did his fear make him act? How do you act when afraid?

2. Do you think it was easy for the wise men to follow the star? Do you think they had any idea what they would find? What brought them joy? Have you ever been on a similar quest?

3. What gifts would you bring the infant Jesus if you were traveling with the wise men?

EPIPHANY

First Sunday after Epiphany
Luke 3:15-17, 21-22

Notes on This Reading

Every year, on this first Sunday after the Feast of the Epiphany, we read the story of Jesus's baptism by John in the wilderness. It doesn't matter which gospel we happen to be reading, because the same story shows up in each of the four gospels. That's a pretty good indication that this is an important story, one that tells us we are supposed to pay attention. Much has been written about why Jesus needed to be baptized. You might want to talk about that. Whatever motivated him, it was clear that it marked the beginning of his public ministry, a ministry that changed the world.

Questions

1. Do you remember your baptism? What do you recall about that event? If you were too young to remember, see if you can locate someone who was present on that great occasion. Let them describe the event. If you don't already do so, find a way to celebrate the anniversary of your baptism each year.

2. Why do you think this story shows up in each of the gospels? Why do you think it is important?

3. Think about that voice that comes from heaven. What does it mean that Jesus was the beloved, and well-pleasing? Have you ever heard that voice speaking to you? (Note: For a beautiful reflection on this voice, read *Life of the Beloved* by Henri Nouwen.)

Second Sunday after Epiphany
John 2:1-11

Notes on This Reading

Here's another story often told at this time of year. It appears only in John's gospel, as the first of many signs that Jesus does, signs that give people an idea of who Jesus is. For that reason, it is a good Epiphany story. The season of Epiphany offers a series of stories that help us see who Jesus is. This is a quirky story, posing as many questions as answers. Why does Jesus seem not to want to perform the miracle? Why is his mother so sure he can do it? Why does he seem to change his mind? Is it just a miracle about catering? Is it more than that? What kind of sign is it?

Questions

1. When have you had an epiphany?

2. What do you imagine Mary thought about her son and his powers?

3. When Jesus says his hour has not yet come, what do you think he means?

4. What do you think weddings represent in the Bible?

5. In what way is this miracle a sign? What does it signify?

Third Sunday after Epiphany
Luke 4:14-21

Notes on This Reading

This Sunday, we return to the Gospel of Luke, and a story only he shares with us. It is about Jesus's inaugural sermon. The story comes in two parts, told this week and next. As Jesus goes to his local synagogue, we get a window on worship in those days. It included a reading from the Hebrew scriptures and a chance for someone to comment on the reading. Jesus reads from the prophet Isaiah, which talks about the liberating power of the Messiah. It sounds like the passage was already selected for him, much as our lectionary guides us from week to week. In one of the shortest sermons in the Bible, Jesus says, "Today this scripture has been fulfilled in your hearing." The sermon may have been short, but it hit home.

Questions

1. Isaiah's readings say that the Spirit has anointed Jesus to do a number of things. Can you list them?

2. How did Jesus do those things throughout his life, and in his death and resurrection? How did he fulfill the prophecy of Isaiah?

3. How does the church, as the hands and feet of Christ in the world, do those same things today? Where do we have growth opportunities?

Fourth Sunday after Epiphany
Luke 4:21-30

Notes on This Reading

This is part two of the story of Jesus's first sermon. Initially, he got good reviews, but then folks started to ask, "Who does he think he is? He's the hometown boy. We know his family. We know what he was like growing up." Jesus notes their resistance and then shares a message found throughout Luke's writing. He says that sometimes outsiders, like the widow of Zarephath or Naaman the Syrian, demonstrate more faith than those who are insiders. (If you want to know more about those characters, they can be found in the Old Testament or Hebrew scriptures. See 1 Kings 17 and 2 Kings 5.) That doesn't sit well with the crowd. In fact, they try to throw Jesus off a cliff. That's what we call a tough sermon review. Jesus miraculously escapes. It is not his time yet.

Questions

1. Why do you think the crowd resisted Jesus's message?

2. Why do you think they got so upset when he talked about the widow or about Naaman? If you are not familiar with those stories, look them up in the Bible.

3. What was it about Jesus that made people want to get rid of him? Is that reaction hard for you to understand?

Fifth Sunday after Epiphany
Luke 5:1-11

Notes on This Reading

This story of the miraculous catch of fish appears in each of the gospels. In the first three gospels, it shows up near the beginning of Jesus's public ministry, as he assembles a group of disciples that will be part of his movement. John's gospel tells this story near the end, as part of the restoration of Peter after his denial, and after Jesus's resurrection. We will read that story this year in the Easter season. It is interesting to note that while many of the disciples were fishermen by profession, there is no record that they can ever catch a fish without Jesus's help. Nevertheless, Jesus calls them and works with them and transforms them into a small group that changed the world.

Questions

1. How do you think the disciples felt when Jesus told them to go fishing when they had failed at it all night?

2. Have you learned more from your failures or from your successes?

3. What do you think Jesus meant when he said: "From now on you will be catching people"?

4. How is God using your gifts and experiences, even those times when you may not have been particularly successful?

Sixth Sunday after Epiphany
Luke 6:17-26

Notes on This Reading

This passage is a portion of teaching Jesus offered to his disciples. In Matthew's gospel, a similar bit of instruction is called the Sermon on the Mount (chapters 5–7). In Luke's gospel, it is called the Sermon on the Plain. A lot of the teaching in these two sermons is the same. Some of it is different. For instance, in Matthew, Jesus says, "Blessed are the poor in spirit." In Luke, Jesus simply says, "Blessed are the poor." Matthew's version is a series of blessings. Luke recounts a series of blessings accompanied by a series of statements that speak of woes, warnings that remind us that Jesus came to comfort the afflicted and to afflict the comfortable.

Questions

1. What do you make of the differences noted between Matthew's and Luke's versions of Jesus's teaching?

2. What's the difference between "Blessed are the poor in spirit" and "Blessed are the poor"?

3. What could possibly be blessed about poverty, hunger, weeping, or having people hate you?

4. What woes come to people who are rich or full or laughing or well regarded? Why should woes come to people in those situations?

5. We noted that Jesus came to comfort the afflicted and afflict the comfortable. Do you agree? Where do you see yourself in Jesus's teaching?

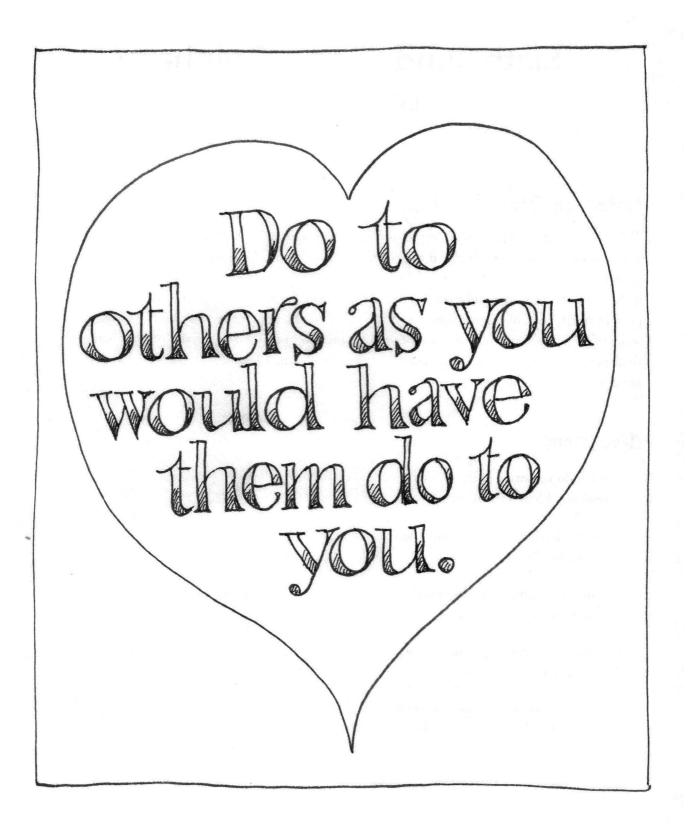

Seventh Sunday after Epiphany
Luke 6:27-38

Notes on This Reading

We continue to read more from Jesus's Sermon on the Plain, which includes the very challenging call to love our enemies. Embedded in this sermon is a teaching of Jesus that is found in some form in most religions. Sometimes called the Golden Rule, it invites disciples—you and me—to treat people the way we wish to be treated. It is not a bad approach in a world marked by division and conflict. We also read about Jesus's teaching on judgment, in which he warns against our tendencies to put ourselves in God's place.

Questions

1. Think of someone you might consider an enemy. What would it mean to show love to them? Are you able to pray for them?

2. We spend our lives making judgments. For instance, you might judge that these gospel drawings are kind of silly or that these questions are dumb. What kind of judging do you think Jesus has in mind?

3. Why does Jesus make such a big deal about forgiveness? Does it sound to you like we will only experience forgiveness if we are able to offer forgiveness? If so, does that make sense to you?

Eighth Sunday after Epiphany
Luke 6:39-49

Notes on This Reading

We have one more opportunity this Sunday to listen to Jesus's Sermon on the Plain. Jesus continues with hard-hitting words, inviting his listeners to pay more attention to their own challenges, rather than to focus on those of other people. He invites self-examination—a look at one's own life to see what kind of fruit it is producing. The sermon ends with a question about the foundation on which we build our lives. Is it one that can withstand challenges, floods rising, and rivers bursting against the house?

Questions

1. What does it mean to be a hypocrite, according to this passage? What can you do to "take the log out of your own eye" before you start with critique of others?

2. What is the difference between hearing the word and acting on it?

3. What is the foundation on which you are building your life? Will it withstand the challenges you face?

Last Sunday after Epiphany
Luke 9:28-36 (37-43)

Notes on This Reading

Every year, on the last Sunday of the season of Epiphany, we read this mysterious story known as the Transfiguration. We also tell this story on the Feast of the Transfiguration, August 6. The first three gospels each tell the story in their own way, but these features are common: Jesus appears in glory on top of the mountain. Moses and Elijah show up, though we are not told how the disciples knew who they were. Peter wishes to freeze the moment in time, but that is not meant to be. A heavenly voice tells them to listen to the Beloved Son, who leads them down the mountain with that awesome experience under their belts, beginning the journey to Jerusalem represented in our tradition as the season of Lent, a journey that will end with Holy Week.

Questions

1. What does it mean that Moses and Elijah show up?

2. How do you imagine the disciples felt throughout this experience?

3. The season of Epiphany begins and ends with a voice from heaven declaring Jesus's belovedness. It first happens when Jesus is baptized, the first Sunday after the feast of Epiphany. What is the significance of that voice?

4. Have you ever heard someone speak of your belovedness?

5. How does this story offer a preparation for the season of Lent?

LENT

Where your treasure is, there your heart will be also. ~Jesus

Ash Wednesday
Matthew 6:1-6, 16-21

Notes on This Reading

On recent Sundays in church, we have heard readings from Luke's gospel that were excerpts from Jesus's Sermon on the Plain. On Ash Wednesday, we always read from a similar sermon found in the Gospel of Matthew, known as the Sermon on the Mount (chapters 5–7). It is a collection of Jesus's teaching that has had great impact over time, especially in the lives of people like Leo Tolstoy, Mahatma Gandhi, and Martin Luther King Jr. This particular passage invites us to enter the season of Lent mindful of how we practice our religion, aware of the temptation to be a hypocrite. In this sermon, Jesus asks his listeners to think about where their treasure might be, because that is where their hearts will be.

Questions

1. Why do you think we read this particular passage at the beginning of Lent?

2. What does this passage tell us about pillars of spiritual practice like prayer and fasting and giving alms? What does it tell us about the way we practice religion?

3. What might it mean to store up treasure in heaven?

4. Think about where you are giving your heart this Ash Wednesday. Are you giving your heart to that which will satisfy your heart?

First Sunday in Lent
Luke 4:1-13

Notes on This Reading

Each of the first three gospels tells the story of Jesus going out into the wilderness for forty days before the launch of his public ministry. In that deserted place, he is tested. Luke and Matthew describe those tests in detail. The first test invites a hungry Jesus to turn stones into bread, to ease that pain with a quick fix. The second temptation invites him to worship the devil and gain power, when Jesus may well have been feeling powerless. The third temptation puts God to the test to see if God would come through in a pinch. The wilderness is not only a place for tests. It is also a place of discovery, a place to be formed into the kind of person God wants us to be. Jesus began his public ministry by facing tests like these. That may well help us when we face tests.

Questions

1. When have you been in the wilderness, either literally or figuratively?

2. What were the challenges? What did you learn?

3. What would be wrong if Jesus had taken the devil up on any of his offers?

4. Shakespeare said that even the devil can quote scripture. He probably had this passage in mind, as Jesus and the devil engage in dueling scripture citation. How do we use scripture in the challenges we face? Do we ever misuse the scripture?

Second Sunday in Lent
Luke 13:31-35

Notes on This Reading

Jesus was not afraid to speak truth to powerful people, religious or political. He did not run from danger, but in the ominous words of the gospels, he "set his face toward Jerusalem." He knew where his journey was headed. As he aimed for Holy Week, we see his loving concern for that holy city, represented in the image of a mother hen trying to gather and protect her children. In this passage, we get a hint of what will come in a few weeks when we celebrate Palm Sunday and Jesus enters his beloved Jerusalem to shouts of hosanna.

Questions

1. What do you think was the secret behind Jesus's courage in the face of Herod's threats?

2. Why is it that we kill prophets? Are we still doing that today?

3. What do you make of the image of Jesus as a mother hen gathering her brood under her wings? Is that a new image for you?

4. What does it mean that the blessed one comes in the name of the Lord?

Third Sunday in Lent
Luke 13:1-9

Notes on This Reading

Jesus is asked to comment on an ancient, perplexing, persistent question: the problem of innocent suffering in the world. Why do bad things happen to good people? He does not offer an easy explanation, because there is none. But noting the randomness of evil, he does not permit any excuse for imagining that our actions are without consequence. So as he often does, he tells a parable to make his point, a parable about the importance of producing good fruit. He speaks in the spirit of the preacher who said God is more concerned with the fruits than the roots.

Questions

1. Do you ever think that bad things happen to folks because they deserve it?

2. Do you wonder about innocent suffering? Have you come up with any answers that have been helpful?

3. One theologian said that in the face of things we can't understand, we are called to withstand. When we can't explain, we proclaim that God is with us. How might you do that? What resources will you draw on?

4. How would you describe the point of Jesus's parable?

5. What does it mean to bear fruit, in a religious or spiritual way? Who in your life has done that?

Fourth Sunday in Lent
Luke 15:1-3, 11b-32

Notes on This Reading

Thanks to Luke, we have this important and widely known parable, often called the Parable of the Prodigal Son, though it is not entirely clear whether the story is about the younger son, the older son, or the father. We read this story on the Fourth Sunday in Lent, a Sunday when the somber mood of Lent lifts a little. It is meant as an explanation of why Jesus chose to meet and greet unsavory folks. At its heart, it is a story about amazing grace and transforming forgiveness. It follows two other parables about being lost and found: a lost sheep and a lost coin. We will read those two stories later in the year.

Questions

1. Who do you identify with in the story, one of the two sons or the father?

2. Look up the word *prodigal*. What does it mean? How does it apply to this story?

3. What lessons do you think Jesus wanted to make in the way that he portrays the father?

4. Have you ever felt like the younger son? Have you ever felt like the older son?

5. How would you describe the Good News (the gospel) in this story?

Fifth Sunday in Lent
John 12:1-8

Notes on This Reading

This story is told a number of times in the gospels, with some differences in the details. In John's gospel we learn that the woman who anoints Jesus's feet is Mary, his good friend from the town of Bethany. It is a beautiful story describing an act of deep devotion. It is also a story that is read on the Tuesday of Holy Week, partly because of the references to Jesus's death. As we near the end of the season of Lent, and anticipate Jesus's death, this story sets the stage for that tale of love and sorrow.

Questions

1. Why do you think Judas resisted this offering made by Mary?

2. What do we learn about Judas from this story?

3. What sense do you make of Jesus's comment about always having the poor with you, but not always having him with you? Does that sound harsh?

4. Does worship seem like a reasonable way to use resources?

Palm Sunday:
Liturgy of the Palms
Luke 19:28-40

Notes on This Reading

Palm Sunday is also called the Sunday of the Passion of our Lord. In other words, there are a lot of themes going on in this one day. Accordingly, we have two passages from the gospel to read in the liturgy of the day. We begin with a parade, a remembrance of Jesus's triumphal entry into Jerusalem, a story told in each of the four gospels in fulfillment of passages in the Hebrew scriptures. The story is a study in fickle human nature, for in just a few days the crowd goes from shouting "Hosanna," an ancient version of hooray, to shouting, "Crucify him." In fact, in our liturgy on this day, we do both those things.

Questions

1. Can you picture yourself in this crowd as Jesus processed into the city on a donkey?

2. Think a bit about that donkey, which was needed by Jesus, and offered by the owners. What might you offer that is needful for Jesus's ministry?

3. What would you make of this apparently spontaneous celebration? Have you ever experienced anything like it?

4. What did Jesus mean that the stones would cry out when the Pharisees, the religious leaders, wanted the public demonstration to stop?

Palm Sunday:
Liturgy of the Word
Luke 22:14—23:56

Notes on This Reading

You have no doubt noted this is a very long reading. It tells the story of Jesus's final days, and is often called the Passion Narrative. The story of these last days is the heart of the gospel. Some have even said that the gospels are really Passion Narratives with long introductions. On this Sunday, as we begin Holy Week, we hear this story. Indeed, we may act it out, as it is often read in parts, like a play. That not only makes it more interesting for the listener, but also makes the key point that each one of us is part of the story. This is not a story about someone else. It is about us.

Questions

1. To which of the characters do you relate in this long narrative?

2. Only Luke tells us about the exchange with the two criminals on the cross, one of which is promised presence with Jesus in paradise. Why do you think that story is included? What would we miss if it were not included?

3. We will read an excerpt from this long Passion Narrative on the last Sunday of the church year, often called Christ the King Sunday. In what sense is Jesus's kingship revealed in this story?

Maundy Thursday
John 13:1-17, 31b-35

Notes on This Reading

As we mark this important day in Holy Week, we join Jesus and his disciples for the Last Supper. We eavesdrop on Jesus's final words to his friends as we read a small portion of a longer address that is found in the Gospel of John, chapters 13–18. Here, Jesus not only talks to his disciples about the call to be a servant and to show love, but he also gives them an example of loving and humbling—and to some, demeaning—ministry by washing their dirty feet. We call this day Maundy Thursday. The word Maundy comes from the Latin *mandatum*, which means command, recalling Jesus's command to the disciples that they love one another and serve one another.

Questions

1. If Jesus knew Judas would betray him, why did he choose him as a disciple?

2. Have you ever experienced betrayal? Have you ever practiced betrayal?

3. Why does Jesus wash the disciples' feet? Why does Peter refuse that ministry?

4. What does Jesus teach his disciples about what it means to be a teacher and Lord?

Good Friday
John 18:1–19:42

Notes on This Reading

Once again, as on Palm Sunday, we have a long reading of the Passion Narrative—in this case, from the Gospel of John. This passage is included, in this or a shorter form, in the Good Friday liturgy. It brings the fourth gospel's distinctive perspective to the story of Jesus's last days. Again, as on Palm Sunday, it offers the opportunity to see what part we play in the story. Throughout the history of the Church this reading has sometimes been used to convey anti-Semitic sentiment too often found in the Christian tradition, so it calls for careful reading and interpretation, as well as a sense of repentance for how scripture has been abused. Included in this passage we find Jesus's encounter with Pilate, which culminates in Pilate's riveting question: "What is truth?" We also hear Jesus's distinctive words from the cross, as he cares for others even as his life is being taken from him.

Questions

1. Judas betrays Jesus and Peter denies him. Do you think one is worse than the other?

2. What do you make of the meeting between Jesus and Pilate? How would you describe both of those characters if this story were all that you knew about them?

3. Is Pilate a sympathetic character in any way? Why?

4. Make a note of all the words Jesus says from the cross. What do they reveal about him?

5. Can you see why this passage has raised questions of anti-Semitism in the history of the Church?

Holy Saturday
Matthew 27:57-66

□ □ □

or John 19:38-42

Notes on These Readings

Here we have two versions of the same story from different gospels. Take this opportunity to compare and contrast them. Note the similarities. This is the only appearance of Joseph of Arimathea in the New Testament. It probably took great love and a measure of courage for him to emerge publicly and ask for the body of Jesus, and then to honor it. He is joined by Nicodemus, whom we meet in the Gospel of John, another rather secret disciple. Their act of devotion helps us realize that there were probably a number of disciples of Jesus that we do not know about. Perhaps that is still the case.

Questions

1. What do we learn about Joseph of Arimathea? What does it mean that he is a secret disciple?

2. How does Nicodemus appear in the version of the story from the Gospel of John? You can also read about his first encounter with Jesus in John.

3. How has he changed over the course of the gospel?

4. What do you think is a good way to observe Holy Saturday?

EASTER

Easter Day
John 20:1-18

Notes on This Reading

We have a choice of gospels for this Sunday, arguably the most important day in the church year. The fact is each of the gospels tells the story of Jesus's resurrection in its own way. There are differences between them, and there are similarities. John is the only gospel that describes the road race to the tomb; Peter and the other disciple are eager to get there to see if the Easter news is true. One of the recurring themes of this new season has to do with the gradual process by which people come to recognize that Jesus is alive. In a variety of ways, even the people who knew Jesus best don't get it at first. That is true for Mary Magdalene, who has a starring role in John's version of the Resurrection. Her encounter with Jesus is powerfully poignant as she recognizes him when he speaks her name. Her grief is broken when he calls to her.

Questions

1. When Peter and the other disciple hear the news that Jesus might be alive, they race to the tomb. Why does the Gospel of John include this story? How does it add to our understanding of that first Easter?

2. Why do you think Mary Magdalene gets such an important role in the Easter story, as she is consistently the first one to get the news that Christ is alive?

3. What do you think kept her from recognizing Jesus at first?

4. What brought her to see that Jesus was alive?

5. What has brought you to see that Jesus is alive?

Easter Day
Luke 24:1-12
(an alternative reading)

Notes on This Reading

Luke's version of the resurrection is different from John's. We don't read the story of Mary Magdalene meeting Jesus in the garden and mistaking him for groundskeeper, but we do repeat the theme that the women are the first ones to see that Jesus is alive, which is in keeping with Luke's interest in highlighting the important role of women in the Jesus movement. Note that the disciples consider the news to be an idle tale, perhaps because they don't grant women much credibility.

Questions

1. What do the resurrection stories have in common? What is different about them?

2. The women make their way to the tomb with one expectation. That expectation is changed. Has that ever happened to you in the journey of faith?

3. One of the themes in these Easter stories is that people do not believe. The disciples at first consider it to be an idle tale. Why do you think that theme is included?

4. Do you think it was harder for those first disciples to believe in the resurrection, or is it harder for us to believe in it?

Easter Evening Service
Luke 24:13-49

Notes on This Reading

Luke is the only gospel writer who tells us about this encounter on the road to Emmaus. Certainly, one of the most touching moments is when one of these disciples explains to Jesus that they had put their hope in the Messiah. As they walk along the road, they are kept from recognizing Jesus, even though in the course of their hike Jesus gives them a wondrous tutorial on the meaning of the Hebrew scriptures. These disciples arrive at their destination and invite Jesus to stay for dinner. Suddenly the guest becomes the host at the table. He breaks the bread and their eyes were opened. They see that their dashed hopes had been resurrected. They hightail it back to Jerusalem to share good news, apparently not even waiting for dessert.

Questions

1. Can you relate to the disciples' experience of disappointment?

2. How have your eyes been opened to see Jesus's presence?

3. Why do you think that their eyes were opened when the bread is broken?

4. Do you see a connection with the Eucharist in this story?

Second Sunday of Easter
John 20:19-31

Notes on This Reading

Every year on this Sunday, after the grand celebration of Easter Day, we read about Jesus's encounter with Thomas of doubting fame. To recognize that doubt, uncertainty, and fear are part of the human experience is an interesting follow-up to the joy of Easter. They are part of the walk of faith. As Frederick Buechner said, "Doubt is the ants in the pants of faith." Thomas has gone down in history as a doubter, but it is worth noting that in his encounter with Jesus he offers one of the greatest affirmations of faith in the gospels, as he says "My Lord and my God." Jesus follows up with a commendation for those who will hear about him through the gospels—that means us. The reading ends with a mission statement about the gospel, which says it is written for a specific purpose: to bring people to believe, and to help people put their trust in the grace of God revealed in Jesus.

Questions

1. Do you understand why Thomas might have doubted? What causes you to doubt?

2. Do you think he gets a bad rap?

3. What are the things that have caused you to believe? What convinces you? What gets in the way?

4. What does it mean to believe? Is it more a matter of the head or the heart?

5. How does belief bring life?

6. How would our faith be diminished if we didn't know this story, told only in the Gospel of John?

Third Sunday of Easter
John 21:1-19

Notes on This Reading

A version of this story of a miraculous catch of fish appears in each of the four gospels. The other three gospels tell this story at the beginning of Jesus's ministry. It is part of his call to follow him. In John's gospel, this fishing story comes at the end—one of the several accounts of the appearance of the resurrected Jesus to his disciples. As is true of many of the resurrection stories, people don't recognize Jesus at first. In this case, with the huge catch of fish, the disciples come to see that Jesus is alive. It leads to an intimate encounter between Jesus and Peter. The one who denied Jesus three times now is invited to restoration, as he affirms three times that he loves Jesus.

Questions

1. Do you see any significance in the disciples returning to their occupation as fishermen?

2. Why do you think the story of catching so many fish is repeated in each gospel?

3. Why does Jesus ask Peter a question three times?

4. What instruction does Jesus give to Peter? Is it the same instruction each time, or does it shift?

Fourth Sunday of Easter
John 10:22-30

Notes on This Reading

The Fourth Sunday after Easter is also known as Good Shepherd Sunday, when our church focuses on the persistent scriptural image that portrays God or Jesus as a shepherd. That theme weaves through the Old Testament. In the New Testament, it is celebrated with special focus in the tenth chapter of the Gospel of John, where Jesus draws on the image of the Good Shepherd in the midst of a controversy with opponents. He claims unity with his Father. The witness to that unity is the series of works he has done.

Questions

1. What do you make of the image of the shepherd? Have you ever felt like you needed one?

2. What kind of shepherd do you need in the midst of controversies?

3. What makes a shepherd good?

4. When Jesus says "My sheep hear my voice," how do you think that voice is heard? Do you ever hear it?

5. As you read this passage, what insights do you get into Jesus's relationship with his Father?

Fifth Sunday of Easter
John 13:31-35

Notes on This Reading

This passage is a short excerpt from Jesus's long farewell address to his disciples, given on the night before he was arrested. It may seem strange to be eavesdropping on the Last Supper during the season of Easter, but Jesus is telling the disciples what he thought was important. As Jesus prepares the disciples for his departure, he gives them a way to keep going. He gives them a new commandment, which is all about love. Love will be the way that people recognize them as his disciples. It will be the way that the Church will grow; in keeping with the words of Presiding Bishop Michael Curry: "If it ain't about love, it ain't about God."

Questions

1. How do you think the disciples were feeling as they gathered for the Last Supper, as Jesus told them he'd only be with them a little longer?

2. How can love be a commandment? Is it a feeling? An action? A decision?

3. How can disciples be recognized? Or, as one preacher put it, if you were arrested for being a follower of Jesus, would there be enough evidence to convict you?

Sixth Sunday of Easter
John 14:23-29

Notes on This Reading

We continue to read excerpts from Jesus's long address to his disciples on the night before his arrest and execution. His speech is found in its entirety in John 13–18. In this portion, Jesus talks about the arrival of the Holy Spirit, an advocate to be sent to the disciples. In other places, that Holy Spirit is described as the comforter. In the Greek, the word for the Holy Spirit is *paraclete,* which literally means "someone who comes along side." This promise comes as an anticipation of the Feast of Pentecost, to be observed in two weeks, marking that time when the Holy Spirit descended on the disciples and the Church was born.

Questions

1. What do you see as the role of the Advocate, the Holy Spirit, in the lives of the disciples?

2. It has been said that on the journey of faith we do not need to be instructed as much as reminded. It sounds like Jesus promises a Holy Spirit who will do both. The Holy Spirit will teach and remind. Recall a time when you were taught about the faith. Recall a time when you have been reminded.

3. When have you felt a need for an advocate, in a spiritual sense or otherwise?

4. What kind of peace is Jesus talking about when he promises peace?

Sixth Sunday of Easter
John 5:1-9
(an alternative reading)

Notes on This Reading

The lectionary gives us a choice for this Sunday that includes another of Jesus's encounters. Relatively early in the Gospel of John, Jesus meets a man who had been sick for many years. We read only a short part of the story, where Jesus asked an important question: "Do you want to be made well?" Jesus does not always ask that question when he meets people in need of healing, but here he does. The man imagined only one pathway to healing. We can imagine that he was filled with despair. Jesus invites him to think about other possibilities. And then he heals him!

Questions

1. What is behind the question that Jesus asks: Do you want to be made well? Are you inclined to think: "Of course the man wanted to be made well"?

2. How do you think the man felt being able to walk after thirty-eight years of paralysis?

3. Have you ever felt stuck in a situation, with apparently no way to make a change? Did the possibility of a change ever scare you?

Ascension Day
Luke 24:44-53

Notes on This Reading

The story of the Ascension is a story that Luke tells twice. It shows up at the conclusion of his gospel and also at the beginning of the Acts of the Apostles. As it portrays Jesus's mysterious ascent into heaven, it answers the question of what happened to Jesus after he was resurrected. The Christian conviction holds that he still lives and reigns. The event also poses big questions for his disciples, including you and me. Specifically, it makes us consider what comes next. Where do we go from here? And who is going with us?

Questions

1. Why is it important that Jesus fulfills the words of the Hebrew scriptures?

2. How do you think the disciples felt as they witnessed his ascent into heaven? What might have been the mix of emotions?

3. The disciples are identified as witnesses. What does that mean? What have they seen?

4. Do you think of yourself as a witness? What have you seen?

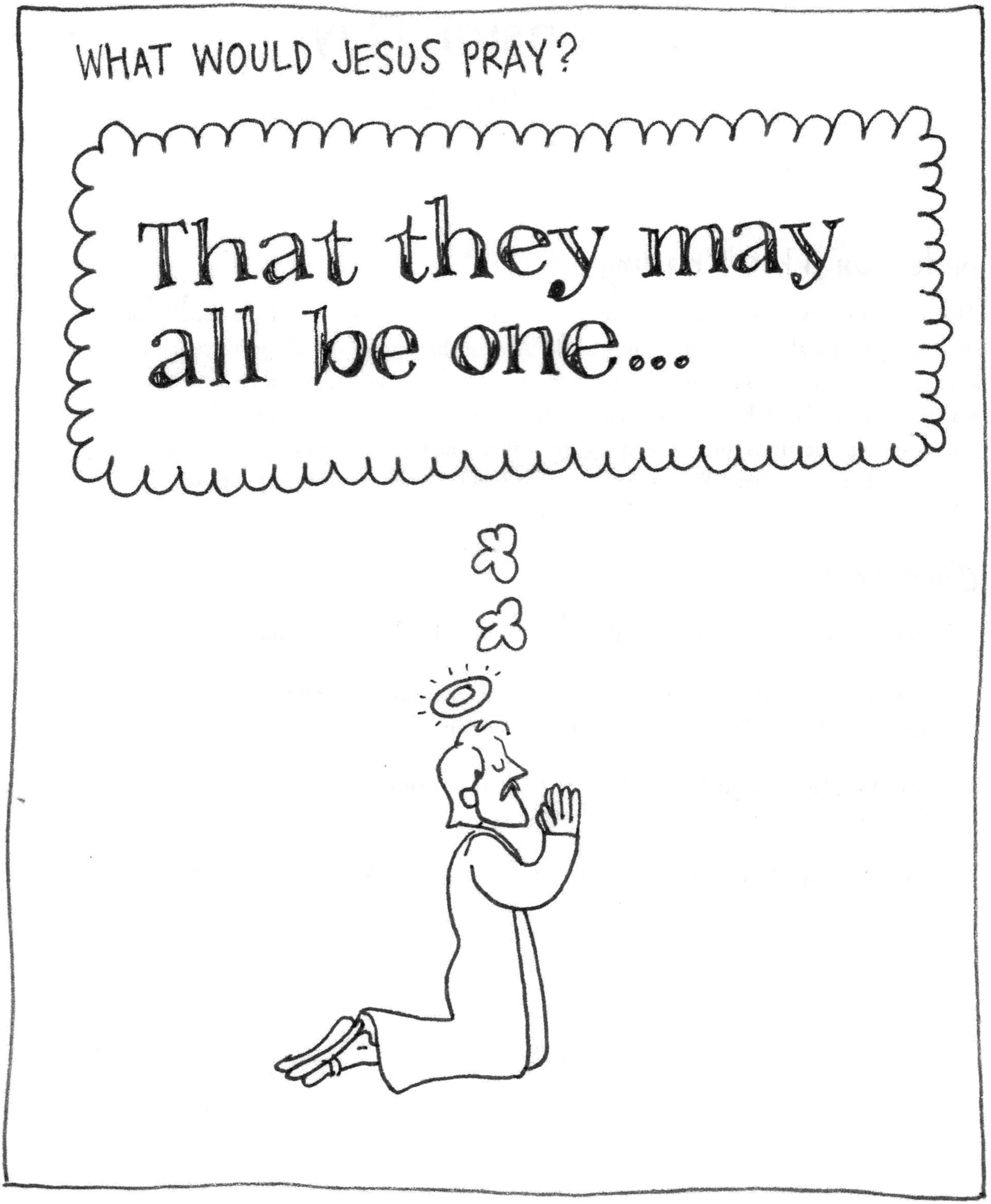
WHAT WOULD JESUS PRAY?
That they may all be one...

Seventh Sunday of Easter
John 17:20-26

Notes on This Reading

Since Ascension Day happens forty days after Easter, it always falls on a Thursday. The Sunday after this feast, therefore, becomes an occasion to remember this important event as the whole community is gathered for worship. On Thursday, we read the story of Jesus's Ascension as told in Luke's writings. For this Sunday, we read a portion of a prayer recorded in John's gospel, offered again on the night before Jesus goes to the cross. The prayer has three parts. Jesus prays first for himself, asking for strength for the impending ordeal. He then prays for his group of disciples gathered with him for the Last Supper, that they will, too, know strength. And then he prays for those who will come to faith through the disciples—those who will come to faith after the Ascension has happened. We include ourselves in that group. What is his prayer for these people? He asks that they all may be one. He ends by asking that the kind of love he has experienced will be experienced by the disciples—a great and powerful prayer.

Questions

1. What would you pray if you were in a situation like Jesus's? What would you ask for yourself? What would you ask for those closest to you? What would you ask for those who in years to come might be affected by your life?

2. When Jesus prays that the disciples will be one, what do you think he is asking? Is he asking for uniformity? For agreement? For absence of conflict?

3. Why do you think Jesus needed to pray at all?

PENTECOST

Day of Pentecost
John 14:8-17 (25-27)

Notes on This Reading

It does not seem that our culture makes a big deal of Pentecost, marketing Pentecost greeting cards or counting the shopping days until Pentecost. There is no Pentecost equivalent of the Easter Bunny or Santa Claus. Yet Pentecost is one of the three big days of the church year. It is called the birthday of the church because it recalls the day when the Holy Spirit ignited the early church, that first group of disciples. Because it is a special day, the illustration for this Sunday is really drawn from the story written in the Acts of the Apostles, which we have cited here.

☐ ☐ ☐

and Acts 2:1-21

Questions

1. Where have you seen the Holy Spirit at work in your own life? In the life of your church? In the world?

2. The Holy Spirit is pictured as wind, as fire, as a dove. What do each of those images suggest about the way the Holy Spirit works? Do you have a favorite among those images?

3. Pentecost has a lot to do with languages. Why is that? How do we communicate the Good News of Jesus to those who may not speak our language, either literally or figuratively?

How would you picture the Trinity?

Trinity Sunday
John 16:12-15

Notes on This Reading

One week after the Feast of Pentecost, the Church dedicates the day to one specific doctrine or teaching. It is the only Sunday during the year that has this kind of focus. It is all about the Trinity, that mysterious doctrine that provides language to describe God as three persons in one. The doctrine developed over the first centuries of the church, though it is suggested or implied in a number of passages in the New Testament. We see the Trinity present in this reading, as Jesus, the Son, speaks to his disciples about what the Father has done, noting the promise of the Spirit that the Father will send. One of the powerful messages in this doctrine is that God is a community. God is about relationship. God is love.

Questions

1. Why do you think it's important that we have a Sunday dedicated to the doctrine of the Trinity?

2. What questions do you have about this doctrine? How might you go about addressing those questions?

3. Read the Nicene Creed and see what it has to say about the Trinity. Imagine you have never read it before. What portions of the creed are compelling for you? What portions are confusing?

4. How would your faith be different if the doctrine of the Trinity was not part of it?

Proper 4
Luke 7:1–10

Notes on This Reading

Now that the celebration of the Easter season has concluded, and we have celebrated the Feast of Pentecost and Trinity Sunday, we return to reading our way through Luke's gospel, our focus this particular year. This gospel will provide readings on Sundays for the rest of the church year, until Advent begins a new church year. There are several things to notice in today's passage. First, the theme of Jesus as a healer comes through loud and clear. Second, we learn about the witness of the centurion. Jesus gives him extraordinarily high marks for his faith, and his ability to trust that Jesus can help him. It is unusual for Jesus, a Jew, to sing the praise of a Gentile, an outsider—and one who served the oppressive ruling class. That is in keeping with the theme of the Gospel of Luke, where outsiders are included in the Jesus movement, where outsiders can be our teachers.

Questions

1. What do you learn about the character of this centurion?

2. What do you think the centurion had heard about Jesus?

3. Why do you think Jesus spoke so highly of him?

4. What does the centurion have to teach us about being a follower of Jesus? What does he model for us? What can you learn from people you might consider outsiders?

Proper 5
Luke 7:11-17

Notes on This Reading

Once again, Luke draws our attention to Jesus as healer. In last week's story, a centurion showed concern for his sick servant. In this story, we feel the intense emotion of a mother, a widow, grieving over the death of her only son. She is in a tough place. She is left all alone. Jesus speaks to her with compassion and says, "Do not weep." He exercises remarkable powers to bring life out of death. It is not surprising that the people respond with fear, nor is it surprising that word about him began to spread.

Questions

1. How do you think the mother was feeling in this situation?

2. Have you ever been at a dead end, similar to her situation?

3. It has been said that compassion is the great virtue common in all faith traditions. What do you think compassion means? When have you seen it at work?

4. What do you make of the crowd's reaction? They fear. They glorify God. They spread news. What do you think is behind each of those emotions?

Proper 6
Luke 7:36—8:3

Notes on This Reading

Jesus had a way of getting into trouble with people in charge. It was a theme throughout his life, as we saw after he gave his first sermon in his hometown of Nazareth. In this story, a woman known to be a sinner enters the house where Jesus is being hosted. The woman expresses her deep devotion to Jesus. The Pharisee criticizes Jesus for it. Jesus calls him out, and holds the woman up as a model of discipleship. The passage ends with a reference, found only in Luke, to the women who were supportive of Jesus. We give thanks to God for the faithfulness of these women.

Questions

1. Why do you think Jesus was so often criticized? What was the Pharisee's objection?

2. Jesus commends the woman for her love, for her deep devotion. What has caused you to grow in love or devotion to Jesus? What may have gotten in the way?

3. Women were often lowly regarded in Jesus's culture. Luke makes a point of highlighting them as models of discipleship. He tells us not only about these women, but also about Mary, the mother of Jesus, Elizabeth, and Anna. What point is he making? How does that point apply today?

Proper 7
Luke 8:26-39

Notes on This Reading

In arguably one of the strangest stories in the gospels, Jesus ventures outside his home territory, maybe even outside his comfort zone, and encounters a frightening man in the grips of demons, many of them, which is what the name Legion suggests. Jesus demonstrates his power over the demons. They are sent into a herd of pigs. The pigs, in turn, accomplish their own destruction. The man, meanwhile, is freed from his torment. He stops terrorizing the local community. He asks to go with Jesus, but instead is told to stay put and tell how much Jesus had done for him. Meanwhile, the local folks ask Jesus to leave.

Questions

1. What is the significance of Jesus venturing into foreign territory?

2. The demons seem to know who Jesus is, better than anyone else. That's true in other places in the gospels. What does that say about Jesus, about the people around Jesus, and about the demons?

3. Why are the demons sent into pigs?

4. Why did the local folks ask Jesus to depart from them? Why did they need him to go away?

5. Why didn't Jesus let the man accompany him? Is it harder to share good news with strangers or with those that you know the best?

6. How do you imagine that the hometown crowd reacted to the change in the man?

Proper 8
Luke 9:51-62

Notes on This Reading

Jesus's journey is not aimless, but is set toward Jerusalem and the central events of Holy Week. Indeed, if this were a movie, the note that Jesus sets his face to go to Jerusalem would be accompanied by ominous, foreboding music. As that journey unfolds Jesus enters into a discussion about the cost of discipleship. He makes it clear that expectations were elevated for his disciples. This journey would demand a great deal from them. Maybe everything. It causes us to consider what it means to be a follower of Jesus.

Questions

1. Often people did not extend a welcome to Jesus. How did his disciples react when that happened? How did Jesus react? What lessons are there for us in Jesus's reaction? How do we feel when people are indifferent or hostile to our own faith?

2. Do you think being a follower of Jesus is easy or hard? What is the cost? What is the promise?

3. What do you think Jesus had in mind when he spoke about not looking back?

4. Have you ever been tempted to look back?

Proper 9
Luke 10:1-11, 16-20

Notes on This Reading

Jesus sends out his disciples with rather specific instructions. Notice he does not send them out alone, but provides companionship for them in the journey. For the most part, it is a call to travel light, to see what God is up to in the neighborhood, and to give up worrying too much about how people respond. He tells his disciples that they will not always be well received. That is not always an easy message to hear. Yet we read that the disciples returned to Jesus with joy, sensing the power that they experienced in sharing Jesus's Good News.

Questions

1. What is the harvest that Jesus is talking about? Who are the laborers?

2. What guidelines for being a disciple do you take from this passage?

3. What does it mean to represent Jesus in the world? How do you feel when the representation is not well received?

4. Where have you seen the kingdom of God coming near to you? What does that look like?

5. When have you experienced the joy of that vision?

Proper 10
Luke 10:25-37

Notes on This Reading

The parable of the Good Samaritan appears only in the Gospel of Luke. Our tradition would be greatly diminished if we did not have this story, which explores what it means to be a neighbor. Thank you, Luke. The story is told in response to a question about what it takes to inherit eternal life. Perhaps that's another way of describing what God wants from us. Jesus responds with the ancient command of his tradition, a command that is simple but not easy, a command that is one thing but actually two. It is all about love of God and love of neighbor. The two are intertwined, and they are best explained in a story like this, a story that focuses on the importance of mercy in our relationships with each other.

Questions

1. What does it mean to love God with heart, soul, mind, and strength?

2. How is love of neighbor related to that?

3. What are the possible explanations for why the priest and the Levite did nothing to help the man who had been beaten? Have you ever had occasion to respond to human suffering with indifference? With fear?

4. Why does it matter that a Samaritan was the one who provided help, becoming the hero of the story?

Proper 11
Luke 10:38-42

Notes on This Reading

Jesus had a few special friends. These sisters were among those who were particularly close to him. If it is true, as some say, that the Bible is a story of sibling rivalry, this passage provides a classic example. Many people find this story to be uncomfortable, and they rise to the defense of Martha. The sisters' different responses to Jesus may suggest different approaches to the spiritual life. They may represent different qualities in the same person. Perhaps there is a bit of Mary and a bit of Martha in each one of us.

Questions

1. Whom do you identify with in this story? Mary or Martha?

2. Do you think Jesus was too hard on Martha?

3. What lessons might you take from this encounter? How would you describe the better part that Mary has chosen?

4. How in your own journey can you choose the better part?

Proper 12
Luke 11:1-13

Notes on This Reading

In this passage, Jesus teaches his disciples about prayer. In response to their request, he gives his disciples a special prayer that will become a mark of their identity. Apparently, John the Baptist had given his disciples a prayer. Jesus's disciples wanted one, too. So he gave them a prayer that appears in every liturgy in the Book of Common Prayer. Here in Luke's gospel we find a shortened version. It may be short and simple, but it covers a lot. Jesus then teaches about the importance of persistence in prayer, a theme we will hear about a few more times in the gospel. All of this talk about prayer is a way of reflecting on our relationship with God.

Questions

1. How did you learn what you know about prayer?

2. What does it mean to ask for daily bread?

3. Why is forgiveness so important in the Lord's prayer? What does it say about us if we refuse forgiveness?

4. Why is persistence important in prayer? When have you had occasion to practice this kind of persistence?

5. Do you think prayer changes God or does prayer change us?

Proper 13
Luke 12:13-21

Notes on This Reading

Throughout his gospel, Luke focuses on the use of money and the lure of possessions. As we have already noted, it has been said that the Bible is a series of stories of sibling rivalry. Demonstrating that there is nothing new under the sun, two brothers come to Jesus arguing over their inheritance. Jesus then tells a parable to make his point, a warning against putting trust in riches, or said another way, a warning against giving one's heart to that which will not satisfy one's heart. It is a challenging message in a world where we measure net worth by what we own, where our lives do in fact often seem to be a reflection of what we possess.

Questions

1. Why do you think Jesus declined to be the mediator in the argument between the brothers?

2. Why do you think he answered with a parable?

3. In what ways do you see people putting confidence in possessions, in treasures? Do you ever do that?

4. What does it mean to you to be rich toward God?

Proper 14
Luke 12:32-40

Notes on This Reading

Jesus continues to focus on treasure, and to encourage his followers to think about what they value. He then talks about being ready and being alert. We heard that theme at the very beginning of the year, in Advent, but it shows up throughout the year. Again and again, New Testament writers will talk about the unexpected arrival—the advent—of the Son of Man. The faithful are encouraged to keep their eyes open, to be prepared for God coming into their lives, maybe even breaking into their lives.

Questions

1. Jesus says that where your treasure is, that is where your heart will be. What does that make you think about what you treasure?

2. Where is your heart these days? Is it pulled in several directions?

3. What do you think it means to be ready for the Son of Man?

4. How might you make that kind of preparation?

5. Has God ever showed up in your life in surprising ways?

Proper 15
Luke 12:49-56

Notes on This Reading

If your only image of Jesus is someone who is meek and mild, Luke wants to change your thinking. Earlier in this year, we noted that Luke seems to buy into the notion that Jesus came to comfort the afflicted and afflict the comfortable. In this passage, he definitely does the latter. He talks about bringing fire to the earth. He talks about bringing division, about bringing the sword, about families being divided. He also continues to counsel his followers to prepare for his arrival, and to look at the signs of the times. Passages like these draw our attention to Jesus as judge. They are not easy or comfortable words, but they are a key part of the story Luke is telling.

Questions

1. In what sense does Jesus bring fire to the earth?

2. What does fire do? What does the phrase "baptism by fire" suggest?

3. Do you think Jesus comes to bring peace, or have you seen how he can bring division?

4. How do you interpret the present time? What do you think God is up to in the world these days? Where do you see God's activity?

5. Would you prefer if Luke had not included this passage in his gospel?

Proper 16
Luke 13:10-17

Notes on This Reading

In the midst of challenging teaching, Jesus encounters a woman who had been imprisoned by a crippling ailment for almost two decades. In keeping with Luke's focus on healing, Jesus sets her free. As is often the case, the work of mercy happens on the Sabbath, violating religious rules of the day. This was no accident on Jesus's part. The authorities criticize Jesus for healing her, but he will not accept their judgment. Instead, he points to the centrality of his ministry of mercy and freedom, doing so with courage as he confronts those in authority and brings healing where it is so desperately needed.

Questions

1. Why do you think that Jesus's ministry as healer gets such emphasis in the Gospel of Luke?

2. What do you think was so important about the Sabbath?

3. Why was it a bad idea to some people to heal on the Sabbath?

4. What is revealed about Jesus's character in this story?

5. What is revealed about the religious leaders of the day? Do these leaders look, in any way, familiar?

Proper 17
Luke 14:1, 7–14

Notes on This Reading

A measure of Jesus's genius is the way he uses parables to make a point that might have otherwise been hard to make. As he watches people continually jockeying for position, Jesus tells stories about banquets. The first story focuses on the call to humility, a warning against self-promotion. The second story issues a call to radical welcome, inclusion, and invitation based not on human measures of merit but on grace alone. Whether in a family, a church, an office, or in the political world, Jesus challenges followers to a new relationship with one another, marked by unconditional love—a rare commodity.

Questions

1. What lessons come to you from the first parable?

2. When have you witnessed genuine acts of humility? How is it possible to develop a sense of humility? How can you practice humility in coming days?

3. When have you experienced the kind of gracious invitation described in Jesus's second story? When have you shown that kind of grace?

4. Where might you be able to offer a more expansive invitation, including someone who has been excluded?

Proper 18
Luke 14:25-33

Notes on This Reading

For those who imagine that Jesus is some ancient Near-Eastern version of Mr. Rogers, passages like this one challenge that notion. Jesus tells the crowd that following him will not be easy. It will not bring peace in families. It will involve counting the cost. He makes no promise that the road will be comfortable. Over the centuries, very few have found it possible to live out his very clear instruction that we give up all our possessions. We can soften his words by saying he did not mean that we should hate family members, or that we should surrender all we have. If everyone did that, where would that leave us? But as he speaks in these striking terms, perhaps speaking in hyperbole, he raises the stakes of being a disciple, and causes us to think about where we are giving our hearts.

Questions

1. What does it mean to carry a cross?

2. What for you is the cost of discipleship? When have you had to pay that cost?

3. What were the rewards when you did?

4. What might it mean to hate family members in order to be a disciple?

5. Did Jesus really expect all of us to give up all our possessions? Are your possessions getting in the way of your spiritual growth?

Proper 19
Luke 15:1-10

Notes on This Reading

In chapter 15 of his gospel, Luke puts together three lost and found stories. Earlier in the year, on the Fourth Sunday in Lent, we read the third of these parables, commonly known as the Prodigal Son. On this Sunday, we read the first two, the story of a lost sheep and the story of a lost coin. These stories are parables of grace and they end in a great celebration filled with the joy of restoration. Go back and reread the whole chapter. When you put them all together, it is a great witness to God's unconditional love, which is worthy of great celebration.

Questions

1. Have you ever felt like a lost sheep? Have you ever searched for something with as much energy as the woman who lost the coin? How did discovery feel?

2. Do you believe that God is searching for us?

3. Do you know people who are like that lost sheep or lost coin? Do you think God can use you in helping to find out where they are?

Proper 20
Luke 16:1-13

Notes on This Reading

If there were a contest of the strangest stories that Jesus tells, this one might be the winner. A dishonest manager is commended for cheating his master. Maybe Jesus knows the story is a bit odd, for he offers an interpretation of the parable, which is something he does not do all that often. The passage ends with a recognition that in life we are pulled in many directions. In the midst of all those competing forces, disciples are called to think about who we serve, and where we find value.

Questions

1. What do you make of the dishonest manager?

2. In what way does he serve as a model of faith, if he does at all? What about him do you think we should imitate?

3. Can you think of a time when you have been faithful in little?

4. Who are you serving in your life these days? Do you have more than one master?

5. Do you ever feel pulled in different directions as parent, child, spouse, sibling, employee, church member, citizen? Where is God in all of that for you?

Proper 21
Luke 16:19-31

Notes on This Reading

This story is told only in the Gospel of Luke. It is a story about economic inequality, an exploration of the great divides that exist between rich and poor. Again, there is nothing new under the sun. The passage also addresses the great chasm between this life and the next. Luke knows that the poor can become invisible. He understands that a sense of entitlement can be a kind of blindness, a very hard habit to break. Take note that the rich man, even in Hades, is still ordering the poor man around. The parable also raises the question of what makes for convincing, compelling belief. All in all, this parable of judgment challenges us to consider what we do with what we are given, an important theme in Luke's gospel.

Questions

1. How would you describe the relationship between the rich man and poor Lazarus during their time on earth? Does that change in the afterlife?

2. Do you ever find as you travel about that some people are actually invisible to you? Do you regard them as valued only because of what they can do for you?

3. What does this parable say to you about wealth? If we enjoy some of it in this life, does that mean we're not to experience it in the next?

4. What convinces people of faith? What made you believe what you believe?

Proper 22
Luke 17:5-10

Notes on This Reading

Jesus continues teaching about faith, implying what has been said in other places: you don't need very much of it to make a difference. Jesus echoes what has been said throughout the gospels, beginning with Mary's response that she was with child. With God all things are possible. Then Jesus moves on to another piece of teaching in which he talks about what it means to be a servant, inviting disciples to recognize their proper role of service and obedience.

Questions

1. In your own spiritual journey, how has your faith increased? What caused that to happen?

2. Have you seen mustard seeds? They're tiny. What does faith the size of a mustard seed sound like to you?

3. When the slave says that we have only done what we ought to have done, what do you think the slave had in mind? What do we owe God? Anything?

4. What part of your faith has to do with a sense of duty or obedience?

Proper 23
Luke 17:11-19

Notes on This Reading

This brief story focuses once more on Jesus's role as a healer. Ten lepers, folks who had little hope of a future in that culture, plead for mercy. They are sent off by Jesus to experience his remarkable healing power. But this healing story is distinctive because it describes the responses of those who were healed. One of the ten lepers who had been healed actually comes back to express gratitude. Only one. That one grateful leper is, of all things, a Samaritan, a despised outsider, ostracized not only by his illness but also by his ethnicity. Once again, Luke offers an unlikely model of faith in the person of an unusual teacher, which is good news for all of us. It means we too can be models of faith, no matter who we are and what we have done or where we are from.

Questions

1. Why do you think it's important that the only one that returns is a foreigner, a Samaritan?

2. Why do you think that the hero of these stories in Luke is often the outsider?

3. What lessons about gratitude do you take from this story?

4. How is the expression of gratitude really an expression of faith?

5. What concrete steps can you take to deepen your sense of gratitude today?

Proper 24
Luke 18:1-8

Notes on This Reading

Luke's gospel has a special focus on prayer. Jesus models the importance of prayer by repeatedly going off by himself to take time to be in conversation with God. In the course of the gospel, Jesus does a fair amount of teaching about prayer, which shows that it is something we can learn, something that deepens with practice—a growth opportunity. This story focuses on the importance of persistence in prayer. Don't give up. If an unjust judge will respond to persistent pleading, how much more will a loving God respond? The passage concludes with a question about whether faith will persist. That's a very good question.

Questions

1. What does it mean to pray always?

2. Paul spoke about praying without ceasing. What do you think he meant by that? How is that possible?

3. Have you had occasion to lose heart in your prayers?

4. What prayers are on your heart that would make you cry out day and night?

5. What made Jesus wonder if the Son of Man would find faith on the earth? Do you ever wonder that?

Proper 25
Luke 18:9-14

Notes on This Reading

Once again, Jesus tells a parable to make his point. And, once again, the Pharisees, the observant clergy of the day, don't come out looking so good. They are the upstanding folks in the community, as is clearly revealed in the way that the Pharisee prays. The tax collector, considered despicable on many levels, has no status in the community, but he experiences justification because of his spirit of humility. There is probably a bit of both of these characters in each one of us.

Questions

1. What does the way we pray say about our view of ourselves and of others?

2. What was it about the prayer of the tax collector that sends him off justified? And what do you think it means to be justified?

3. Is it possible to pursue humility as a goal, or does it just kind of happen?

4. Once you're aware of humility in yourself, have you lost it?

Proper 26
Luke 19:1-10

Notes on This Reading

This story, humorous in many respects, offers important lessons about what an encounter with Jesus might be like. Zacchaeus, short of stature and apparently short of friends, wishes to see Jesus but perhaps wishes to do so in a surreptitious way. Jesus discovers his hiding place, calls him out, and invites himself over to Zacchaeus's house, where in short order, a conversion takes place. A new way forward opens up for Zacchaeus. He experiences a big change because he meets Jesus. It affects the way he lives his life, the way he uses his money, the way he treats other people, the way he seeks to make amends for damage he has done. He makes amends because he has a personal encounter with Jesus.

Questions

1. If you were filming this story, who would you cast as Zacchaeus?

2. What does this story tell you about Jesus?

3. Why do you think Jesus was criticized for going to Zacchaeus's house? Do you think he cared?

4. What impresses you most about the changes that came to Zacchaeus?

5. When have you had a change of heart that caused a change in relationships?

Proper 27
Luke 20:27-38

Notes on This Reading

Trick questions are nothing new. Jesus presides at a first-century press conference and leaders ask him a question that defies a winning answer. The question reveals a lack of imagination on the part of the questioners. Jesus calls them to a broader vision, with a promise of resurrected life that is beyond their limited concepts or logic.

Questions

1. What do you think Jesus's questioners were after? What was their goal in posing this question about the seven brothers?

2. What does it mean to you that Jesus points to a God of the living and not a God of the dead?

3. As you ponder puzzling questions (and the world presents a lot of them), where would you be helped by a greater sense of imagination?

Proper 28

Luke 21:5-19

Notes on This Reading

As we approach the end of the liturgical year, the tone in the readings is marked by an ominous foreboding. The disciples marvel at the beauty of the Temple, an amazing human accomplishment. Jesus notes the temporal nature of such accomplishments. He warns of a challenging road ahead. He doesn't sugarcoat it. It is not going to be easy. But he also promises the disciples that they will not be abandoned, no matter how hard life gets. His promise to those first disciples is a promise we can take to heart in the challenges we face. We are not alone.

Questions

1. What Jesus describes seems terrifying, suffering on a cosmic and individual level. Have you every experienced that kind of terror?

2. When you hear what lies ahead for the disciples, do you ever wonder why they continued to follow Jesus?

3. When in your life have you needed to show endurance? What resources did you summon to help you practice endurance?

Proper 29
Luke 23:33-43

Notes on This Reading

This is the last Sunday of the church calendar year. It is often referred to as Christ the King Sunday. Each year, the gospel reading will ask some version of this question: Exactly what kind of king was Jesus? In this year of reading Luke's gospel, we meet Jesus in the final hours of his life, in his brutal torture and death. Even in these hours, it is notable that he is focused on others. Luke is the only gospel writer that includes this poignant conversation with the other criminals on the cross. Our tradition would be diminished if we did not hear the comforting words of Jesus to the thief, "Today you will be with me in paradise." His words are a response to the thief's plaintive request, "Jesus, remember me." It is a beautiful way to conclude our liturgical year, with a prayer to Jesus and a promise of his presence for all time.

Questions

1. What does this passage say about Jesus's character?

2. If you were in Jesus's place on that cross, do you imagine you'd be talking about forgiveness?

3. Why do you think Luke included the conversation that took place among those three being crucified?

4. How did the two criminals who were crucified with Jesus regard Jesus? What made the difference between the two?

5. In what sense do you regard Jesus as a king?

IN CONCLUSION

It has been a privilege to take on this project. After years of preaching on lectionary texts, the opportunity to reflect on the whole year brought me to a new and refreshed gratitude for the life and ministry of Jesus. His healing presence shines through these passages. As these readings have spoken to me in new ways, I hope and pray that they will move your heart as well.

—The Rev. Jay Sidebotham

I love to tell the story of unseen things above,
Of Jesus and his glory, of Jesus and his love.
I love to tell the story because I know it is true
It satisfies my longing as nothing else can do.
I love to tell the story, 'twill be my theme in glory,
To tell the old, old story of Jesus and his love.

I love to tell the story for those who know it best
Seem hungering and thirsting to hear it like the rest,
And when in scenes of glory I sing the new, new song,
'Twill be the old, old story, that I have loved so long.
I love to tell the story, 'twill be my theme in glory
To tell the old, old story of Jesus and his love.